tao te ching

the poetry of nature

Also by the same author:

The Mind's Mirror: Dream Dictionary and Translation Guide
The Mythology of Sleep: The Waking Power of Dreams
Nothing Bad Happens in Life: Nature's Way of Success

tao te ching

the poetry of nature

By Kari Hohne

Published by Way of Tao Books.
P.O. Box 1753 Carnelian Bay, Ca 96140
PaperBird is a division of Way of Tao Books.
www.wayoftao.com
Printed in the United States of America

ISBN 978-0-9819779-3-5

For Alan, my lotus flower in the river of change.

Contents

Introduction

"While carrying on
with life in your head,
can you embrace its mystery
and not let go?"

These are the words of the Tao te Ching, an ancient text that celebrates *the art of living*. Fostering an appreciation for a more natural way of being in the world, this classic work is inspired by the order observed in nature. Each poetic verse displays the timeless wisdom of simplicity. When we can trace our seamless unity with everything that unfolds around us, we discover both the purposefulness and the mystery of Tao. This beautiful work is made all the more profound because it comes to us from antiquity.

"Through compassion, one can triumph in attack"

Although this book came to advise rulers about the strategy of managing an empire, it is obvious that its ideas allow one to find a subtle peace in existence. Unlike other Eastern philosophies, Taoism does not deny existence. It teaches one to understand and flow with the changes.

The ancient Chinese philosophers knew that *"when you open all obstacles disappear."* In any type of conflict, compassion always ensures a win/win situation that leads to triumph.

The Tao te Ching explores nature's movement toward productive growth and regeneration and reveals how the human journey is no different. All living things follow an *inborn* pattern of development, coaxed forward by the changes taking place in the environment.

> *"I dare not play the host*
> *but prefer to be the guest."*

Approaching each experience as a guest and appreciating how something mysterious is always unfolding, one discovers meaning and purpose in daily life. Playing the host with a mindset of expectation and control, one discovers how *"those who go against the way end up being called unlucky."* It is better to follow where the changes may lead us.

> *"You can mould clay into a vessel;*
> *yet, it is its emptiness that makes it useful."*

In order to be open to growth, *"one that remains open can be newly filled."* In time, all things come to us because the way is ever purposeful. Even the most difficult situations always lift us into a higher level of being.

> *"Those with misfortune cannot understand the reason for their loss.*
> *The sage does not make distinctions,*
> *embraces everything and remains open."*

Recognizing our tendency to live in the future and to ignore the ever changing moment, its repetitive theme ever asks us to remain open and pliable in all we do.

"When you have little,

contentment is simple.

When you have too much, you are perplexed."

"To be a valley to the empire" is to be open and nurturing to others. In discovering how one is *"fed by the mother,"* we honor the Way for what it might teach us.

Like a seed that holds within the potential of becoming an oak, experience peels away our protective layers so that we can move toward actualization. Inspired by the ways of nature, there are no limits to what we may become because life is always exploring the best of what it might be.

Te, or the principle of Tao active in each creature resembles our idea of individuation or evolution. This driving and activating force is the more ancient idea and philosophical root of Qi or Ch'i. Our need for conformity can lead us away from our center, although experience always returns us to our authentic nature. The Tao te Ching is therefore, translated to mean a *book that cultivates te when one follows Tao.*

The ancient Chinese respected nature as a teacher. Emulating its ways, water taught one about the power of stillness. As it meets an obstacle, it grows in volume and energy to overcome any barriers to its forward progress. Fire offered a lesson about synergy and interdependence. We discover how the inner flame is always connected to whatever keeps it burning. The Mountain provided perspective, or how constancy revealed a type of order. The Lake inspired a powerful peacefulness, regardless of the changes taking place upon its surface. In its depths, was a perpetual stillness and the source of its wellspring. *"When one becomes lost, one must only return to stillness."*

At the same time, the seasons changed with the sound of Thunder. Observing the oppositional forces that worked to bring about change in the natural world, nature demonstrated productive growth through friction. Without this oppositional energy, the ancient Taoist recognized how life would lose its vitality to become stagnant.

Therefore, a sage was always a student of nature. When obstacles became insurmountable, one simply emulated the way of nature. The Tao te Ching becomes a study on how to return to our state of simplicity as natural creatures in a natural world.

"The ordinary person puts themselves
in the center of the universe;
the universe for the sage, is always at the center."

The ancient masters studied eight principles of change as the natural world moved toward renewal. These primary forces are at the root of a more ancient text called the *I Ching* or Book of Changes. Each principle portrays a virtue to be emulated when approaching a world of perpetual change. With nature as our teacher, we discover a pathway of empowerment, happiness and success. We find that in the Great Circle there is no separation between the world *in here* and the world *out there.* *"Everything is already complete in oneself."* One need only open to the changes to allow experience to bring our real nature forward.

The writing of the Tao te Ching has been attributed to Lao Tzu, a contemporary of Confucius and keeper of the imperial archives at Loyang, in the province of Honan, during the 6th century BC. According to legend, he was riding away into the desert, sickened by the ways of men when a gatekeeper persuaded him to record his wisdom. Scholars have traced its threads in the many writings of the ancient Chinese philosophers, who were in turn, also inspired by the Book of Changes. Therefore, some believe that this text was a compilation of ideas brought together during the 3rd century BC.

This text attempts to provide an idea of what Tao is, since it does not lend itself to clear cut interpretation. Lao Tzu taught that since Tao is ever changing, it cannot be captured in words. This version of this ancient classic captures its original poetic style, and is a compilation drawn from the many agent sages who studied it.

The ancient Chinese poets made an art form out of capturing nature existing "just so." The second section of the book includes Taoist poetry, inspired by nature and celebrating what is timeless and valuable about our existence.

The Study of Nature

There is a dynamic force driving all things towards evolution, and this force is active even in human events. The Tao te Ching describes life's fundamental interconnectivity: *"there is a thing confusedly formed."* We observe this when nature orchestrates plant reproduction by utilizing seeds that attach to the fur of passing animals. Pollen grains are transferred on the legs of tiny insects, while the delicate construction of arbor seeds harness the wind for regeneration.

Carnivores eat herbivores, eliminating nutrient rich waste that nourishes the plants. Bacteria process this waste, enriching the plants that nourish the herbivores. Water is stripped of nutrients by flowing through a filter of complex root structures before entering the pristine reefs that nourish the sea creatures. Human beings ward of viruses, bacteria and disease by ingesting the exoskeletons of coral animals and sea creatures.

As animals exchange carbon dioxide for oxygen, plants trade oxygen for carbon dioxide. Every species thrives because of its interdependence upon another. Each can exist in a foreign environment and yet, at some level every environment is connected. This all or nothing equation fosters harmony at all levels of life.

At the same time, we see mating collisions, eruptions and positive and negative forces that collide to turn the wheels of evolution. At the molecular level and in opposing pressure systems, we see how nature releases stagnation through a type of friction. Evolution is how life achieves renewal by removing the protective covering of the past. All that appears to block our forward progress will lift us to a higher level of existence.

We can discover our deeper connection to what unfolds around us when immersed within nature's rejuvenating tapestry of colors and sounds. While the natural world reminds us of the things that remain constant over time, it also teaches us about the necessity of remaining open to change.

Nature is blind to barriers, except in the way that it overcomes them. Observing its diverse processes, we discover these same evolutionary mechanisms also lead us in our growth.

Exploring the best of what it might become, nature fine tunes existing traits, while eliminating what is outworn and unnecessary. More importantly, it is relentless in its ability to overcome any barriers to its forward progress. Over and above how nature renews our senses, the Tao of Nature teaches us about balance, wellness, and how *"success is a pathway of self-completion."*

Like the seedling forced to press against the dirt and rocks to peel away its protective covering, all obstacles simply remove what hides our authenticity.

8

Tao is at the root of everything that happens in the world. By following the path of least resistance, one allows life to take its natural course without interference. This is at the heart of the Taoist idea of "not doing." *"Without doing anything, nothing is undone."*

We become *"the master of our present existence"* in our simplicity of perspective. We *"do not play the host, but become the guest"* and strive to be open and observant. *"Composure will straighten out one's inner life."* This willingness to meet life half way reflects the composed state of our inner world upon experience. Becoming the master of our experiences requires only that we follow. Exerting the will against events will only create further obstruction as we move upon the great river of life.

> *"I alone am inactive and reveal no signs;*
> *like a new-born babe who has not learned to smile,*
> *Unattached, as though I have no home to go back to."*

The home we would have gone back to is the paradigm that would trap us in our growth.

Part One

Tao te Ching

In The Great Mystery

1

The Tao that can be spoken of is not the constant Tao.
The name that can be named is not the constant name.

The nameless is the beginning of life.
It is the mother of the ten thousand things.

Remove your desires and you will see the mystery.
Be filled with desire
and you will see only the manifestation.

These two are the same
yet, they diverge in nature
as they issue forth.

Being the same, they are the source
but the source remains a mystery.
Mystery upon mystery,
the gateway of Tao's manifold secrets.

All Things Are Equal

2

All people measure beauty
against what they know to be ugliness.
All announce that good is good
only because they reject what they think is bad.

Therefore, something and nothing produce each other.
The difficult and the easy compliment each other.
Long and short influence each other.
High and low arise from each other.
Notes and tone harmonize with each other.
Before and after always follow one another.

Thus, one on the pathway of discovering te
acts without striving
and teaches without words.
Deny nothing to the ten thousand things.
Nourish them without claiming authority,
benefit them without demanding gratitude,
do the work, then move on.

And, the fruits of your labor will last forever.

Hold To Nothing

3

Not seeking credit, the talented avoids rivalry.
Not seeking what can be owned
prevents stealing.
Not displaying desirable things
prevents the confusion of the heart.

Therefore, one of Tao governs by
emptying the heart of desire
and fills the belly with food,
loosens ambitions
and strengthens the bones.

If the people are simple and free from desire,
then the empire will be at peace
of its own accord.

Practice action without striving
and all will be in order.

Soften the Glare

4

Tao is like an empty vessel,
yet use will not drain it.
Never needing to be filled,
it is the deep and unfathomable source
of the ten thousand things.

Blunt the sharpness.
Untangle the knots.
Soften the glare.
Settle like dust.
Let your wheels move only along old ruts.

Darkly visible,
it only seems as if it were there.
I know not its name.
It existed before the ten thousand things.
I call it Tao.

Hold Fast to Emptiness

5

Nature is indifferent to life.
It treats all creatures equally
without thought to what must pass.
The truly wise understand its ways.

The universe is like a bellows:
empty, yet quite full and never exhausted.
The more it works, the more comes out.

Many words lead to exhaustion.
Better to hold fast to emptiness.

Dimly Visible, Yet Present

6

Yin is like a valley that is always present.
It is the unknown first mother,
whose gate is the root of all things.

Dimly visible, it only seems as if it were there.

Draw from it all you wish;
it will never run dry.

17

Detached and At One

7

The Yin and Yang are old and last forever.
It is because they are without distinction
that they endure.

The truly wise put the person last;
and find they are at the forefront.

What is not guarded will always be preserved.

One that is detached is one with all.

Without thought of the self,
one still accomplishes their private ends.

Settle Anywhere

8

Highest good is like water.
It benefits the ten thousand things without striving.

It settles in places that people avoid
and so is like Tao.

In choosing your home, look to the land.
In preparing the mind, go deep.
In associating with others, value gentleness.
In speaking, exhibit good faith.
In governing, provide good order.
In the conduct of business, be competent.
In action, be timely.

When there is no strife, there is nothing to be undone.

Never Full

9

Rather than fill anything to the brim
it is better to have stopped in time.

You can sharpen a blade
but its sharpness will not last forever.
You can fill your house with precious jade
and you will be forced to guard it.

Demonstrate pride and arrogance
and you will invite your downfall.

Retire when the work is done.
That is the way of Tao.

The Mysterious Mirror

10

While carrying on with life in your head
can you embrace its mystery in your arms,
and not let go?

While giving full expression to your vital force
can you make it pliable like that of a newborn babe?

While polishing your mysterious mirror
can you see the world without blemish?
While loving and leading the people
can you do so without interfering?

When the great gate opens and shuts
can you keep to the role of the female?
What is closed will always be made open.

While penetrating the four quarters with your insight
can you still remain simple?

Help all things grow and nourish them.
Yet lay no claim or authority.
Benefit others without seeking gratitude.
Guide them, yet do not control them.

This is the power of mysterious Virtue.

Return to the Center

11

Thirty spokes share the hub of a wheel;
yet it is its center that makes it useful.

You can mould clay into a vessel;
yet, it is its emptiness that makes it useful.

Cut doors and windows from the walls of a house;
but the ultimate use of the house
will depend on that part where nothing exists.

Therefore, something is shaped into what is;
but its usefulness comes from what is not.

Nourish the Belly, Not the Eye

12

The five colors interfere with seeing.
The five notes confuse the ear.
The five flavors dull the palate.

Searching always drives the heart wild with excitement.
Goods that are hard to obtain lead one astray.

Therefore, the truly wise
nourish what is for the belly and not the eye.

They reject the "that" to lay hold of the "this."

Without Distinctions

13

The ordinary person seeks good fortune, and avoids misfortune,
cherishes success and avoids failure.
These distinctions are like the body.

Good fortune comes to startle as much as when it is taken away.
Those with misfortune cannot understand the reason for their loss.

The sage does not make distinctions,
embraces everything and remains open.
The ordinary person puts themselves
in the center of the universe;
the universe for the sage, is always at the center.

Thus, the sage views the world as their larger body
and are best suited to care for the world;

they love humanity as they love themselves
and can be entrusted with the world.

The Form of the Formless

14

Look for Tao and it cannot be seen; it is invisible.
Listen and it cannot be heard; it is inaudible.
Reach for it, although it cannot be touched; it is intangible.

What is unfathomable can only be looked upon as one.

It rises like illumination, but does not dazzle.
It settles back down, but is not obscure.
It is without beginning, and end,
It is infinite, indefinable.

This is the form of the formless;
it exists in non-existence;
Being indefinable
is its greatest mystery.

Go up to it, and you will not see its beginning;
follow behind, and you will not see its end.

Hold close to the ancient Tao
and become the master of your present existence.

The ability to know the beginning of antiquity
is the thread running through the way.

So Subtle and Profound

15

The ancient masters of Tao:
So wise, so subtle, and profound.
So deep in their understanding,
that they were themselves misunderstood;

They were:
Tentative, like crossing a stream in winter;
Hesitant like one aware of danger;
Courteous, like a visiting guest;
Subtle, like the melting of ice;
Simple, like the uncarved block;
Vacant, like a valley;
Obscure, like muddy water.

Who can be muddled and settling slowly
become clear?
Who can remain still and stirring slowly
come to life?
Move too hastily and it becomes clouded again.

One who holds fast to the way
does not wish to be full.

Because one is never full
they are worn, and yet can be newly made.

Return to Stillness

16

Go to the end of emptiness.
Hold fast to the way of stillness.
The myriad things all rise together
and return to their separate roots.

Returning to your roots is called stillness.
Returning to stillness reveals your nature.
Returning to your nature, you will discover the constant.

Knowing the constant is called enlightenment.
Not knowing the constant leads to difficulty.

Knowing the constant leads to openness.
Openness leads to impartiality.
Impartiality leads to kingliness.
Kingliness leads to the divine;
The divine leads back to Tao
and Tao to perpetuity.

Know this,
and to the end of your days
you will meet with no danger.

It Happens Naturally

17

The best of all rulers is but a shadow to the people.
The next best ruler is loved and praised by them.
Next is the ruler who is feared.
And finally, there is the ruler that the people despise.

Without trusting how can one be trusted?

The wise lead the people by following behind.

When the task is accomplished and the work done
the people all say:
"it happened to us naturally."

Without Wisdom

18

When the great Tao is forgotten
there is benevolence and justice.

When the people are wise
the great deception begins.

When family relationships are not in harmony,
filial piety and parental devotion are advocated.

When a country falls into chaos and disorder,
there is only the praise of loyal ministers.

Without Knowledge

19

Throw out wisdom and abandon knowledge;
The people will benefit a hundred times.

End benevolence; abandon righteousness
and the people return to filial praise.

End cunning; discard profit;
Robbers and thieves no longer exist.

These three things are external and inadequate.

People need what they can depend on:
reveal simplicity; embrace the natural;
control selfishness; reduce desires.

I Alone am Inactive

20

Give up learning and put an end to your troubles.
How much difference is there between yes and no?
How much difference is there between good and evil?
Should I fear what other people fear?
How very remote the actual occurrence!

The people of the world make merry
as though making a sacrifice or
ascending the hills in a springtime festival.
I alone am inactive and reveal no signs;
like a new-born babe who has not learned to smile,
Unattached, as though I have no home to go back to.
The people have more than enough.
I alone seem to have nothing.
Muddled, I remain indiscriminate and nebulous.
While others are full of knowledge.
I alone am simple and dull.
Most people see differences and are sharp.
I alone make no distinctions,
Calm, like the sea;
like a restless wind that never ceases.
People of the world all have a purpose.
I alone seem impractical and out of place.

I alone am different from others,
and value being fed by the Mother.

How Do I Know?

21

In every movement
one of great virtue follows Tao and Tao alone.

Tao is elusive and intangible.

Intangible and elusive, yet within it is an image.
Elusive and intangible, yet within it is a form.
Deep and obscure, yet within it is an essence.
The essence is very real, and therein,
is something that can be tested.

From the ancient times until now,
its manifestations have never ceased.

It is that by which we may see the beginning of all things.
How do I know what is at the beginnings of all things?

Because of this.

Contentment is Simple

22

Bowed down, you are preserved.
Sometimes bent, you are made straight.

When you are empty, you are made full.
When you are worn, you can be newly made.

When you have little, contentment is simple.
When you have too much, you are perplexed.

Therefore the wise embrace the One
and become an example to all.

They do not display themselves and are therefore visible.
They do not justify themselves and are therefore great.
They do not make claims and are therefore given merit.
They do not seek glory and can therefore endure.

Because they do not contend,
nothing contends with them.

Is not the ancient saying true?
When you bow down, you are preserved.

Turning back, you are preserved to the end.

Conform to Nature

23

Nature says very little.
A strong wind does not last all morning,
and a downpour cannot last all day.

If even Nature's utterances do not last long,
how much less should be that of human beings?

That is why one follows the way of nature.
Those who know only the Way conform to the Way.
Those who know only virtue have virtue.
Those who know only loss conform to loss.

Those one with the Way are embraced by the Way.
Those one with the power of virtue take comfort in virtue.
Those one with the loss experience loss willingly.

If one has not learned to trust
how can they be trusted?

Only Harmony Endures

24

Those standing on tiptoe appear unsteady.
Those walking too hastily cannot maintain the pace.

Those who must explain themselves are not clear.
Those who make a show of themselves are not distinguished.

Those focused on only glory cannot be useful.
Those at one with Tao know that what is not useful does not endure.

Like food in the body, what is unnecessary is eliminated.
Thus, those who possess Tao have no use for that.

There Is A Thing Confusedly Formed

25

There is a thing confusedly formed;
Born before heaven and earth.
In the silence, it is the void.

Ever alone and unchanging,
goes round and round and does not weary.
It is the mother of all things.
I know not its name.
To speak of it, I call it "Tao."

Forced to describe it, I call it "great."
Being great, it is described as receding.
Receding, it is described as far away.
Being far away, it is described as turning back.
Therefore the Tao is great
What is above is great
What is below is great
The ruler is also great.

There are four greats in the universe
And the ruler counts only as one.
Humans follow the laws below;
What is below follows the laws of above.

What is above is orchestrated by Tao
and Tao is the law of nature.

The Root of The Light

26

The heavy is at the root of the light.
Stillness is the master of restlessness.

Therefore the sage, traveling all day,
does not lose sight of what is carried.

Though there is great beauty to be seen "out there,"
one is unattached and ever composed "in here."

What should happen if the lord of ten thousand chariots
acts lightly in the world?

To be light is to lose one's root;
To be restless is to lose one's sense of stillness.

Use No Counting Rods

27

When you are traveling, leave no tracks.
When you speak, know when to stop.

One who measures needs no counting rods.

The proper door needs no lock,
yet cannot be opened.
The proper binding needs no knot,
yet cannot be untied.

Therefore the sage cares for others,
And does not abandon anyone.

Caring for everything,
they abandon nothing.
This is the way of enlightenment.

Therefore the good is the teacher the bad learns from;
and the bad is the material the good works with.

Not to value the teacher
and to disregard the material,
One may be intelligent, though they are greatly confused.

This is called the essential mystery.

Return to the Uncarved Block

28

Know the male, but hold to the role of the female.
Be like water that nourishes the valley.

Being the watercourse for the world,
the endless virtue will not run dry
and you will return to the state of innocence.

Know purity, but hold to the role of darkness
and be an example to the world.

Being an example to the world,
the endless virtue is unwavering.

And you will return to the boundless and infinite.
Know honor, but keep to the role of the disgraced
and be the valley to the world.

Being the valley of the world
the endless virtue will be sufficient.

Return to being the uncarved block.
When it is carved, it becomes useful.
Because the sage is useful,
they become great leaders,

Thus the greatest cutting does not sever.

It Cannot Be Contained

29

Can you take power over life and control it?
It cannot be done.

It is the composition of a sacred instrument,
and requires no improvement.

If you try to control it, you will ruin it.
If you try to hold it, you will lose it.

Some things lead and some things follow.
Like the breath, you cannot hold it.

Some things are hard and some things are supple.
Some things climb to take by force, only to fall.

Therefore the sage:
Avoids extremes
eliminates excess and arrogance.

Force Is Not Necessary

30

If you would counsel a ruler on the way of Tao
teach how force is not necessary.
To conquer others only brings forward their resistance.

Where there is an army, brambles grow
and in the wake of a mighty army,
bad harvests follow without fail.

A good leader achieves success by knowing when to stop.
Achieves followers without the use of domination.

They know success, but do not brag;
They achieve results, but are not arrogant.

They achieve results because it is the natural way.

Results come by way of necessity
and not through force.

Force exhausts strength.
and is not the way of Tao.

That which goes against the way
will come to an early end.

Value Turning Back

31

Weapons are tools that destroy
and all things detest them.
Therefore, those who possess Tao do not need them.
The wise value turning back,
while others would push blindly forward.

Weapons are tools that destroy;
They are not the tools of the wise.
They are used when all else fails
and victory offers no cause for rejoicing.
Calm detachment can be more powerful.

Those who seek glory
may delight in the killing.
Those who delight in killing
will never know the value of life.
Auspicious events favor those who turn back;
Inauspicious events favor those who push blindly forward.

In the army, the lieutenant stands to the left,
while the general is positioned to the right.
This is how people stand at a funeral.

Those who have been killed
are mourned with sadness.
Victory during war is like a funeral.

Know When to Stop

32

Tao is forever nameless and unformed.

In its simplicity, it cannot be grasped.
If you could harness it,
the ten thousand things would follow on their own.

What is above and what is below
move in harmony to bring about rain and dew.

Without the use of force,
all things are nurtured, but unaware.

When the whole is divided, it has names.
These names come to exist everywhere.
As soon as there are names,
you should know that it is time to stop.

Knowing when to stop,
you can be free of danger.

Tao is to the world,
like stream to the valley
that always flows back to the sea.

Whether Strength or Weakness

33

Those who understand others are intelligent;
Those who understand themselves are enlightened.

Those who overcome others have force;
Those who overcome themselves are strong.

Those who know contentment are rich;
Those who persevere have purpose.

To remain still is to endure;
To die but not to perish is immortality.

Tao Claims No Authority

34

The great Tao flows everywhere;
It can flow to the left or to the right.

The myriad of things depend on it, yet it claims no authority.

It achieves its work, but does not lay claim to merit.
It clothes and feeds the myriad of things, but makes no claim
of being their master.

Ever desiring nothing it might be called insignificant.

The myriad of things return to it, but it does not control them.
In this, it can be called great.

Because it does not seek greatness,
it succeeds in achieving greatness.

Used, Yet Not Exhausted

35

Have in your hold the great image,
and the empire will come to you.

Coming to you and meeting with no harm,
it will be safe and sound.

Music and food may induce the wayfarer to stop
but the way of Tao passes through the mouth
without flavor.

It cannot be seen
and cannot be heard;

Although you use it, it cannot be exhausted.

The Nature of Things

36

If you would have something shrink,
you must first stretch it.

If you would weaken something,
you must first strengthen it.

If you wish to lay something aside,
you must first set it up.
If you wish to take something,
you must first learn to give it.

This is called subtle clarity,
and seeing into the nature of things.

The soft and the weak overcome the hard and strong.

Just as the fish has no need to leave the deep water,
the sharpest weapon does not need to be displayed.

Nothing is Undone

37

Tao invariably takes no action,
and yet, there is nothing that is left undone.

If a leader understands this,
the myriad of things will transform on their own.

After transformation, should desire raise its head,
they are restrained naturally,
by the weight of the nameless uncarved block.

The uncarved block is undefined simplicity,
and is the freedom from desire.

Without desire there is only stillness.

Through non-action,
the empire will be at peace of its own accord.

The Beginning of Disorder

38

Highest virtue is unaware of being virtuous.
Therefore, one has virtue.

Inferior virtue tries to be virtuous.
Therefore, one has lost their virtue.

Highest virtue never acts
yet, there is nothing left undone.

Inferior virtue is always doing something,
and yet, there is much that is left undone.

Highest benevolence means taking action
with no ulterior motive.

Highest righteousness strives to take action
but has an ulterior motive.

Highest discipline means taking action
but when there is no response,
rolls up the sleeves
and resorts to taking by force.

Therefore when the Way is lost,
virtue becomes important;
when virtue is lost, the way of benevolence rises;
when benevolence is lost, the way of morality rises;
when morality is lost, the way of ritual becomes important.

Now, ritual is a superficial expression
of the slow loss of loyalty and faithfulness,
and the beginning of disorder.

Those who see something on the horizon
may think that it is Tao flowering;
when it is actually the blossoming of folly.

Therefore the wise dwell in the thick
and not in the thin;
are nourished by the fruit, and not the flower.
The sage discards "that" to take hold of "this."

Using the Inferior as a Base

39

Those that attained oneness since ancient times:
The sky attained oneness and thus became clear.
The earth attained oneness and thus became settled.
The gods attained oneness and thus became potent.
The valley attained oneness and thus abundance.

The myriad of things attained oneness and thus life.
The lords attained oneness and became rulers.

It is the One that makes these what they are.
The sky, lacking clarity, soon thunders apart.
The earth, lacking tranquility, is soon shaken.
The gods, lacking potency, soon wither away.
The valley, lacking water, soon dries up.
The myriad of things, lacking life, would perish.
The lords, lacking understanding, would soon fall.
Therefore, the superior must have the inferior as a root;
The high must have the low as a base.
Thus the rulers call themselves alone, desolate, and unworthy.
This is using the inferior as base? Is it not so?

Therefore, supreme praise is without praise:
Not wishing to be among others glittering like a precious jewel,
nor to be too aloof, like a piece of stone.

It Turns Back

40

Turning back is how the way moves.
Weakness is the means the way employs.

The myriad of things in this world are born from "something"
although "something" comes from "nothing."

Forward and Backward

41

The wise hear of Tao and do there best
to practice it.

The average person hears of Tao and
they sometimes keep and sometimes lose it.

When the inferior person hears of Tao
they laugh out loud at it.

If they did not laugh, it would not be worthy of being Tao.

Therefore we say the following:

The way that is brightest seems dull.
The way that leads forward seems to
lead backward.
The way which is even seems rough.

Highest virtue is like a valley.
Great purity appears sullied.

Far reaching virtue appears insufficient.
Active virtue seems inactive.
Solid virtue appears unsteady.

The great square has no corners.
The great vessel takes long to complete.

The great music is imperceptible in sound.
The great form has no shape.

Tao is hidden in being nameless.

Yet it is Tao alone, which excels in bestowing;
and brings all things to completion.

It Produces the Two

42

Tao is the One.
It produces the two: Yin and Yang.

The Two produce the three,
and the Three produce the ten thousand things.

The creatures carry on their back the unknown Yin,
that they may embrace in their arms, the essential Yang.

All things are the blending of the generative
forces of the two.

No creature wants to be thought of
as insignificant, powerless or unworthy.
Yet, the masters use these terms to describe themselves.

So with all things,
some things gain by being diminished
and other things diminish when they are added to.

What the ancients taught
I also teach:
"The use of force and violence brings a violent end."

I will use this as the principal of my teaching.

The Most Submissive

43

The most submissive thing in the world
can ride roughshod over the hardest thing.

That which has no substance
enters into that which has no crevices.

From this I know the benefit of taking no action;
This is the teaching without words that few understand.

Know When to Stop

44

Which is dearer: the person or the title?
Which is more valuable: one's own life or wealth?

Which is worse: gain or loss?

Thus excessive desire leads to great spending.
Excessive holding leads to great loss.

One who knows contentment suffers no disgrace.

Knowing when to stop; you will meet with no danger.
Therefore, you can long endure.

Great Fullness Seems Empty

45

Great perfection will always appear chipped,
but its usefulness will not wear it out.

Great fullness seems empty
but its usefulness is inexhaustible.

Great straightness seems bent.
Great skill seems clumsy.
Great eloquence seems inarticulate.

Restlessness always overcomes the cold
while stillness always overcomes the heat.

Without doing anything,
you can become the leader of the empire.

If You Are Content

46

When Tao prevails in the world
fast horses are retired to plough the field.

When Tao does not prevail in the world,
warhorses give birth on the battlefield.

There is no greater crime than having too many desires.
There is no greater uneasiness than a lack of contentment.

There is no misfortune greater than greed.

If you are content,
you will always have enough.

Without Going Out the Door

47

Without going out the door, one can see the whole world.

Without looking out the window, one can see the way of Tao.

The further one goes,
the less one knows.

Therefore, the sage
knows without going
Understands without looking
and accomplishes without taking action.

Order Returns To the World

48

In the pursuit of learning, you learn more each day.
In the pursuit of the way, you do less each day.

You do less and less, until you take no unnatural action.

Even though no action is taken, nothing is left undone.

Order always returns to the world through non-interference.
The one who interferes is not qualified to be a leader.

Thus Goodness Grows

49

The sages have no mind that remains their own,
they take the mind of the people as their mind.

Those who are good, are treated with goodness.
Those who are not good, are also treated with goodness.

Thus, goodness grows in the empire.
Those who are honest are treated honestly.
Those who do not know honesty are still treated honestly.

Thus, the virtue of honesty grows in the empire.

The sage, in an attempt to distract the mind of the people
will seek urgently to muddle them.

Giving them something to entertain their ears and eyes,
they are treated like children.

You Come In and Go Out

50

You come into life, and go out in death.
Three and ten are your companions in life.

Three and ten are your companions in death.

Three and ten are also those companions
that value life and so, bring death.

How is this so? Because these are the organs and orifices
that are worn out by the intensive striving after life.

I've heard that one who is good at preserving life
will not encounter wild buffalo and tigers.

And in fighting, will not try to escape the weapons of war.

The wild buffalo have no place to thrust its horns.
The tiger has no place to clasp its claws.

Weapons of war have nowhere to penetrate.

How is this so? Because there is no part of them
that is worn out by the intensive striving against death.

The Way Gives Them Life

51

The way gives them life,
virtue raises them.

Things give them shape
and circumstances bring them to maturity.

Therefore, all things respect Tao and value virtue.
They rely on Tao to develop virtue,
not because it is decreed.
They know that it is natural
that they should be cared for.

Thus the way gives them life,
virtue raises them.

Circumstances nourish them;
Tao protects them and brings them to maturity.

It gives them life
but does not possess them;
Benefits them without seeking gratitude.

Guides them, but does not rule over them.

This is called Mysterious Virtue.

The World Has a Beginning

52

The world has a beginning.
This beginning is like the mother of all things.

When you know the one as the mother
you will come to know her children,
in the myriad of things.

Knowing her children,
go back to holding fast to the mother,
and to the end of your days,
you will live without danger.
Close the mouth and eyes;
shut the doors of desire.
And all that you need will never run dry.
Open the mouth and eyes;
meddle with your desires.
And all that you take will not fulfill you.

Seeing what is small is called enlightenment.
Being submissive, you find strength.
Utilize the light
but give up discernment.
And thereby avoid calamity.

This is called following the constant.

The Great Way is Easy

53

If I had but little knowledge
I should, when walking on the broad way,
fear only the paths that lead astray.

The great way is easy,
yet people prefer the by-paths.
The courts are exceedingly splendid,
The fields are barren with weeds.

The granaries are exceedingly empty;
Yet some are dressed in fineries.

They carry swords at their sides,
have their fill of food and drink.

Possessed of wealth, they are extravagant
this is called taking the lead in the robbery.

This is indeed not the way of Tao!

To Know the Person

54

That which is firm cannot be uprooted.
That which is strongly held cannot be taken.

From generation to generation, they will commemorate it forever.

Cultivate it in your person; its virtue will be genuine.
Cultivate it in the family; its virtue will be overflowing.
Cultivate it in the community; its virtue will be lasting.
Cultivate it in the country; its virtue will be abundant.
Cultivate it in the world; and its virtue will be universal.

Therefore, to understand the person, observe what one cultivates.

Observe the family by what it cultivates.
Observe the community by what it cultivates.
Observe the country by what it cultivates.
Observe the world by what they cultivate.

How can I know the world?

By means of this.

If The Grasp Is Firm

55

Those who have virtue in abundance
are similar to a newborn babe.

Poisonous insects do not sting them;
Wild beasts do not claw them.
Birds of prey do not attack them;
Their bones are weak, their tendons are soft
But their grasp is firm.

They do not know of sexual union but can manifest arousal.

When your essence is at its height,
you can roar all day and not become hoarse.
This is because your natural harmony is unobstructed.

Knowing harmony is said to be the constant.
Knowing the constant will lead to clarity.
Trying to avoid one's vitality will lead to danger;
A mind overusing the vital force becomes aggressive.

If it reaches its height it can be exhausted
although being exhausted is contrary to Tao.

Therefore, that which goes against the way
will come to an early end.

Those Who Know – Untangle The Knots

56

Those who know do not speak.
Those who speak do not know.

Block the openings;
Shut the doors.
Blunt the sharpness;
Untangle the knots.
Soften the glare;
become one with the dusty world,
and let your wheels move along old ruts.

This is called Mysterious sameness.
To be like this:
Others can neither be intimate nor indifferent to you.
Others can neither benefit nor harm you.
No one can honor or disgrace you.

Therefore, you are honored by the way.

Remain Simple Like an Uncarved Block

57

Govern with upright integrity and correctness.

You deploy the military with surprise tactics
but you would have the world by not meddling.

How do I know this is so?
Through this:
The more taboos and restrictions there are in the world,
the poorer will be the people.

The more sharp weapons are given to the people
the more troubled the empire will be.
The more cunning and skill the people possess,
the more vicious these things will appear.
The more the laws are posted in the city,
the more robbers and thieves will exist.

Therefore the sage says:
I take no action, and the people of themselves are transformed.
I prefer stillness, and the people of themselves find solutions.
I do not interfere, and the people of themselves become prosperous.
I have no desires, and the people of themselves become simple.

They remain simple, like an uncarved block.

The People Have Not Been Perplexed

58

When the government is complicated
the people become simple.
When government searches and scrutinizes,
the people become shrewd and crafty.

Misfortune is what fortune perches upon;
Beneath fortune, misfortune is hiding.

Who knows where one ends and the other begins?
They have no determined outcome or limit.

Rightness reverts to become crafty.
Goodness reverts to become wicked.

The people have not been perplexed
for many long days.

Therefore the sage is:
Straight like the square that does not scrape.
Incorruptible as a blade that does not cut.
Extending out, but not at the expense of others.
Shines bright, but does not dazzle.

Having Nothing to Overcome

59

In governing and serving
be sparing.

Only by conserving do things recover quickly.
Recovering quickly means one is following the way.

Accumulating virtue means there is nothing one cannot overcome.

When there is nothing that one cannot overcome
no one knows the limits.

The limitations being unknown, one can possess greatness.
In possession of Tao, one can endure.

This is called the way of deep roots and a firm stem.

It is the Tao of longevity and lasting vision.

With Care That Does Not Harm

60

Ruling a large country is like
the special care required to cook a small fish.

Apply the subtleness of Tao to rule the empire,
with similar care that does not harm.

Not that one remains powerless,
but since it is good , it does not harm the people.

Not only does the good not harm the people
the sage also does not harm people.

They both do no harm to one another
and each receives the merit of the other's virtue.

The Converging Point of Many Streams

61

The large country is like the lower part of a river.

It is the converging point of many streams
and the place where things unite.

The female always overcomes the male with softness.
Being yielding, she takes her place beneath him.

Therefore if a great country gives way to a smaller country,
it will conquer the smaller country.
And if a small country submits to a great country,
it can conquer the great country.

Therefore, those that would conquer must yield,
and those that conquer, accomplish by being yielding.

A great nation wants to take the other under its wing;
and the smaller country want sits services to be accepted.
So that each gets what it wants and finds the proper place,
it is correct that a great nation yield and take the lower position.

The Place Where the Bad Finds Refuge

62

Tao is the treasure house of all things.

It is the treasure of the kind person
and the place where the bad finds refuge.

Admirable words might win you respect;
Admirable actions can raise you above all others.

Even if one is bad,
should they be abandoned?

Therefore, when crowning the Emperor
and installing the three ministers,
although there is the offering of jade before four horses
why not kneel and be seated in Tao?

Why did the ancients value Tao so much?
Did they not say: "those who seek always find;
And those with guilt can find freedom?"

Therefore, it is the greatest value in the world.

Approach the Difficulty While it is Easy

63

Do that which consists in taking no action;
Pursue that which will not be meddlesome.
Savor what cannot be described by flavor.
Make what is small, big; what is few, many and
respond to hatred with virtue.

Approach the difficult while it is still easy.
Deal with the big while it is still small.
The difficult tasks of the world
must be handled by starting what is easy.

Great undertakings must always start with what is small.
Therefore, the sage never strives for the great,
thus they achieve greatness.
One who makes promises lightly does not have faith.
One who takes things too easy may encounter much difficulty.
Therefore, the sage regard things as difficult,
and therefore, encounters no difficulty.

The Transition is Easy

64

What is still in transition, is easy to change.
When it shows no signs, it is easy to mould.

When it is still fragile, it is easy to break.
When it is still small, it is easy to dissolve.

Deal with something while it is still nothing;
Keep it in order before disorder sets in.

A tree as big as a man's embrace
grows from a tiny shoot.

A tower of nine levels
starts from a heap of earth.

A journey of a thousand miles
begins and ends beneath one's feet.

The one who meddles with the way will ruin it,
The one who holds fast to the way, will lose it.

Therefore, the sage does nothing and nothing is ruined.
By not laying hold of anything, nothing is lost.

People, in handling affairs
often come close to completion and fail.
If they were as careful in the end as in the beginning,
then they would not have failed.

Therefore, the sage desires not to desire.
They do not value goods that are hard to acquire.

They learn to unlearn;
They redeem the faults of the people
to assist in bringing their nature forward,
but do not interfere.

Knowledge Can Rob Enlightenment

65

In ancient times, those who practiced Tao well
used it not to enlighten the people
but to return them to simplicity.

The difficulty in governing people
comes when they have been excessively trained.

Therefore, one knows that knowledge can become
the robber of enlightenment.

One that can lead the people
with something beyond knowledge,
will be a blessing to the state.
Know that these two are both standards.
Always knowing these standards
is called profound and secret Virtue.

Virtue is deep and far-reaching!
When all things return to their natural state
it turns back with them.
Only then is harmony reached.

Tao Pushes Them Tirelessly

66

Rivers and oceans can take from mountain rivers
because they naturally stay below.

So they can be the kings of a hundred valleys.

Thus if the sage wishes to lead the people
they must, in their words,
place themselves below.

If they wish to be in front of people
they must, in their person, follow behind them.

Thus the sage is positioned above
but the people do not feel burdened.
They are positioned in front
but the people feel no obstruction.

Thus Tao pushes them forward tirelessly.

Because they do not contend
so the world does not contend with them.

What the Way Provides

67

Everyone in the world says that my Tao is vast
and resembles nothing.
It is because it is vast that it
resembles nothing; if it resembled anything
it would have, long ago, become small.
I have three treasures,
which I hold and protect:
The first is called compassion;
The second is being malleable like an uncarved block;
The third is not daring to take the lead in the empire.
Being compassionate, one can afford to be courageous.
Being malleable, one is able to extend oneself outward.
Not daring to take the lead in the empire,
one is able to become a leader.

Now if one has courage but discards compassion;
Reaches widely but discards being malleable;
Goes ahead but discards being behind,
this is fatal.
Through compassion, one can triumph in attack
and be impregnable in defense.

What the way provides during times of need,
it protects with the gift of compassion.

One Has No Need to Engage

68

The greatest warrior is not formidable;
The skillful fighter has no need to get angry.

Those who are good at achieving victory, have no need to engage.
Those who are good at managing people place themselves below.

This is called the virtue of non-contention.
It is called strength.

This is the ultimate sublimity of Tao.

I Dare Not Play the Host

69

The strategists say:
I dare not play the host, but prefer to be the guest.
I dare not advance an inch, but prefer to withdraw a foot.

This is called marching forward when there is no road.

Rolling up the sleeve, where there is no arm.
Dragging the adversary about when there is no adversary;
it is like holding weapons when there are no weapons.

There is no greater disaster than believing in enemies
this almost made me lose my treasure.

So when two sides raise their arms against each other
it is the one that is sorrow-stricken who will win.

My Words Have an Ancient Beginning

70

My words are easy to understand and easy to practice.
There are few who can understand and practice them.

My words have an ancient beginning.
and my actions stem from principles.

People do not understand this.
Therefore they do not understand me.

Those who know me are few;
thus I am highly sought.

Therefore the sage, while dressed in plain clothes
conceals his person like a valuable piece of jade.

To Know But To Think You Don't Know Is Best

71

To know but to think you don't know is best.
To not know but think you know leads to difficulty.

By being aware of difficulty, one can avoid it.

The sage meets with no difficulty.

Being aware of difficulty,
nothing is difficult.

They Will Follow Naturally

72

When people lack a sense of awe,
  often calamity falls upon them.

Do not intrude into their places.
  Do not upset their livelihood.

Because you do not interfere,
  they will follow naturally.

Therefore the sage:
Knows but does not glorify themselves.
Respects but does not praise themselves.

Thus they discard the one
  to take hold of the other.

Who Knows What Heaven Dislikes

73

The bold in daring will be killed
The bold in not daring will survive.

Of these two, one brings benefit, the other brings harm.

Who knows why Heaven dislikes what it dislikes?
Even the sage finds this a difficult question.

The way of Tao:
It does not contend and yet excels in winning.
It does not speak and yet excels in responding.
It does not summon and yet attracts.
It is unstructured and yet excels in planning.

The net of heaven is cast wide,
though the mesh is not fine, nothing slips through.

The Great Carpenter Cuts

74

People do not fear death.

How can they be threatened with death?

If people are made to constantly fear death
then those who act unlawfully
might be captured and killed,
but who would dare?

There exists a master executioner that kills.
To undertake killing for the master executioner
is like substituting for the great carpenter to cut.

Those who substitute for the great carpenter to cut,
it is rare that they do not injure their own hands.

Those That Do Not Seek After Life

75

The people's hunger
is due to the excess of their ruler's taxation
so they starve.

The people's difficulty in being governed
is due to the meddling of their ruler,
so they are difficult to govern.

The people's disregard for death
comes from the way
the ruler pursues life so vigorously.

It is only those that do not seek after life
that excel in making life valuable.

Be Supple and Pliant

76

While alive, the body is soft and pliant.
When dead, it is hard and rigid.
All living things, grass and trees,
while alive, are soft and supple
When dead, they become dry and brittle.

Thus that which is hard and rigid
is on the pathway of death.
That which is soft and yielding
is the follower of life.

Therefore, an inflexible army will not win.

A strong tree will not suffer the axe.

The big and forceful occupy a lowly position
while the soft and pliant occupy a higher place.

The High it Brings Down

77

Is not the way of heaven
like the stretching of a bow?

The high it brings down
the low it lifts up;
It takes from what is in excess,
in order to make good of what is deficient.

The way of heaven
reduces what is in excess,
in order to give
to what is deficient.

The Tao of the people is not so.

They reduce further those that are lacking,
and offer more to those who already have.

Who can offer to others what they have in excess?

Only those who have the Tao.

Therefore the sage benefits, but seeks no gratitude,
gives but without taking credit.
They do not wish to display their virtue
and still their virtue shines forth.

Straightforward Words Seem Paradoxical

Nothing in the world is softer or weaker than water.
Yet nothing is better than water
at overcoming the hard and strong.

For this reason, it has no substitute.

That the weak overcomes the strong
and the soft overcomes the hard,
everybody in the world knows
but cannot put into practice.

Therefore the sage knows:
The one who accepts the humiliation of the state
can be its master.
The one who accepts calamity in the state
becomes its ruler.
Straightforward words seem paradoxical.

How Can This Be Good

After settling a great dispute
there must be remaining resentments.

How can this be considered good?

Therefore the sage holds the due part of the contract
but does not demand payment from the other person.

Those who have virtue hold to a contract.
Those without virtue hold to collections.

The way of Tao has no favorites.
It is always on the side of the good.

Let the People Return

80

If you make the country small and
give out many weapons
with no need to use them;
the people will be reluctant to migrate to other lands
because they know that death is no light matter.

Although they have boats and chariots
they have no need to use them.
Although they have armor and weapons
they have no need to display them.

Let the people return to using the knotted rope,
savoring their food, admiring their clothes,
content in their homes, happy in their customs.

Neighboring countries see one another,
hear the sounds of roosters and dogs from nearby lands.

The people, until they grow old and die
have no need to go to the other.

To the Tao

81

Truthful words are not beautiful.
Beautiful words are not truthful.

Good words need no persuasion.
Persuasive words are not good.

One who knows has no extensive knowledge;
One broad of knowledge does not know.

The sage does not hoard.

Even while bestowing everything to others,
there is yet even more.

Although they give everything to others,
they are richer still.

The Tao of heaven
benefits and does not harm.

The Tao of the sage
is bountiful and does not contend.

Part Two

Taoist Poetry

You will discover
the germinating power of te
in the silence
where a thousand seeds
are becoming the landscape of spring.
Way of Tao

"I asked the boy beneath the pines.
He said: the Master's gone alone
herb picking somewhere on the mount,
cloud-hidden, whereabouts unknown."

Jia Dao

"Joy and anger,
sorrow and happiness,
caution and remorse
Come upon us by turns,
with ever changing mood.

They come like music from hollows,
like wood when played by the wind,
or how mushrooms grow from the damp.

Daily and nightly they alternate within,
but we cannot tell whence they spring.

Without these emotions I should not be.
Without me, they would have no instrument."

Chuang Tzu

"In front of my bed, the moonlight shone.
For a moment, I took it for frost on the floor.
When I lifted my head, I saw that it was the Moon.
When I bent my head, I dreamt of my far-away home.'
Li Po

"A flock of birds fly high in the distance,
A lonely cloud drifts idly on its own.
We gaze at each other, neither growing tired,
There is only Jingting Shan Hill."
Li Po

Winter/Spring

"Bears, dragons, tempestuous on mountain and river,
Startle the forest and make the heights tremble.
Clouds darken beneath the darkness of rain,
streams pale with a pallor of mist.
The gods of Thunder and Lightning
Shatter the whole range."

Li Bai

"Slowly autumn comes to an end.
Painfully cold a dawn wind thick with dew.

Grass round here will not be green again,
Trees and leaves are already suffering.
The clear air is drained and purified
And the high white sky's a mystery.

Nothing's left of the cicada's sound.
Flying geese break the heavens' silence.
The Myriad Creatures rise and return.
How can life and death not be hard?"

Tao Qian

"Beneath the light, the river and hills are beautiful,
The spring breeze bears the fragrance of flowers and grass.
The mud has thawed, and swallows fly around.
On the warm sand, mandarin ducks are sleeping."

Du Fu

"The water murmurs
in the old stone well,
And, a rippling mirror,
gives back the clear blue sky.
The river roars,
swollen with the late rains of spring.
On the cool, jade green grass
the golden sunshine
splashes.

Sometimes, at early dawn,
I climb
even as far as Lien Shan Temple.
In the spring
I plow the thirsty field,
that it may drink new life.
I eat a little,
I work a little,
each day my hair grows thinner,
and it seems,
I lean ever a bit more heavily
on my old thornwood cane."

Liu Tzu-Hui

Spring/Summer

"I slumbered spring's morning and missed the dawn
from everywhere, I heard the cry of birds.
That night the sound of wind and rain came.
Who knows how many petals had fallen?"

Meng Haoran

"A little child paddles a little boat,
Drifting about, and picking white lotuses.
He does not know how to hide his tracks,
And duckweed's opened up along his path."

Bai Juyi

"Make your heart like a lake
with a calm, still surface
and great depths of kindness."

Lao Tzu

"An early cicada chirps and is silent;
The flickering candle sinks and brightens.
Outside my window, I can hear the evening rain
By the sound it makes on the banana leaf."
Bo Juyi

"A path that starts where the clouds end,
And springtime is as long as the pure stream.

Sometimes flower petals fall
And flow distantly on the fragrant water.
Facing the mountain trail, the idle door
Of a library deep among the willows.

In this mysterious place, the sun shines every day
Her bright beams reflect on my robes."
Liu Shen Xu

Summer/Autumn

"A strip of water's spread in the setting sun,
Half the river's emerald, half is red.

I love the third night of the ninth month,
The dew is like a pearl; the moon like a bow."
Bai Juyi

"The autumn hill gathers the remaining light,
A flying bird chases after its companion.
The green color is bright
And brings me into the moment,
like a sunset mist that has no fixed place."
Wang Wei

"Autumn clouds, vague and obscure;
The evening, lonely and chill.
I felt the dampness on my garments,
But saw no spot, and heard no sound of rain."
Po Chu-i

"I burned incense, swept the earth, and waited
for a poem to come...

Then I laughed, and climbed the mountain,
leaning on my staff.
How I'd love to be a master
of the blue sky's art:

see how many sprigs of snow-white clouds
he's brushed in so far today."
Yuan Mei

"There is a narrow, sunless path that leads to the temple tree,
Deep and dark, it is covered in abundant green moss.

Wait by the gate when you are finished sweeping the yard,
By chance you might see a monk coming down from the hill."
Wang Wei

Autumn/Winter

"In the third month of autumn it blows down the leaves
to open up the second month's flowers.
On the river are waves of a thousand feet.
Among the bamboo, ten thousand are dry and slanting."
Li Qiao

"Wind passes over the lake.
The swelling waves stretch away
without limit. Autumn comes with the twilight,
and boats grow rare on the river.

Flickering waters and fading mountains
always touch the heart of man.
I never grow tired of singing
of their boundless beauty.

The lotus pods are already formed.
And the water lilies have grown old.
The dew has brightened the blossoms
of the arrowroot along the river bank.

The herons and seagulls sleep
on the sand with their
heads tucked away, as though
they did not wish to see
the men who pass by on the river."
Li Ch'ing Chao

"Two monks sit facing, playing chess on the mountain,
The bamboo shadow on the board is dark and clear.
Not a person sees the bamboo's shadow,
One sometimes hears the pieces being moved."
Bai Juyi

"The plants all know that spring will soon return,
All kinds of red and purple contend in beauty.
The poplar blossom and elm seeds are not beautiful,
They can only fill the sky with flight like snow."
Han Yu

"Then as without the touch of verse divine
There is no outlet for the pent-up soul,
'Twas ruled that he who quaffed no fancy's bowl
Should drain the "Golden Valley" cups of wine."
Li Po

"A dog's bark amid the water's sound,
Peach blossom that's made thicker by the rain.
Deep in the trees, I sometimes see a deer,
And at the stream I hear no noonday bell.

Wild bamboo divides the green mist,
A flying spring hangs from the jasper peak.
No-one knows the place to which he's gone,
Sadly, I lean on two or three pines."
Li Bai

"The universe is but a tenement
of all things visible. Darkness and day
the passing guests of Time.
Life slips away,
a dream of little joy and mean content.

Ah! wise the old philosophers who sought
To lengthen their long sunsets among flowers,
By stealing the young night's unsullied hours
And the dim moments with sweet burdens fraught.
And now Spring beckons me with verdant hand,
And Nature's wealth of eloquence doth win
Forth to the fragrant-bowered nectarine,
Where my dear friends abide, a careless band.

There meet my gentle, matchless brothers, there
I come, the obscure poet, all unfit
To wear the radiant jewelry of wit,
And in their golden presence cloud the air.

And while the thrill of meeting lingers, soon
As the first courtly words, the feast is spread,
While, couched on flowers 'mid wine-cups flashing red,
We drink deep draughts unto The Lady Moon.

Then as without the touch of verse divine
There is no outlet for the pent up soul,
Twas ruled that he who quaffed
No fancy bowl
Should drain the Golden Valley's cups of wine."

Li Po

108

"

"Through the evening mist a lone goose is flying.
Of one tone are wide waters and sky.
The hills are shadows
And they flow from form to form
And nothing stands."
Unknown

"Over the river, the shining moon;
in the pine trees, the sighing wind.
All night long, so tranquil – why? And for whom?"
Unknown

Meditations

"I divined and chose a distant place to dwell
T'ien-t'ai; what more is there to say?

Monkeys cry where valley mists are cold,
My grass gate blends with the color of the crags,
I pick leaves to thatch a hut among the pines,
Scoop out a pond and lead a runnel from the spring.

By now I am used to doing without the world,
Picking ferns, I pass the years that are left."

Hanshan

"The trail to Cold Mountain is faint
the banks of Cold Stream are a jungle

birds constantly chatter away
I hear no sound of people
gusts of wind lash my face

flurries of snow bury my body
day after day, no sun
year after year no spring."

Hanshan

"The leaf tips bend
under the weight of dew.

Fruits are ripening
in Earth's early morning.

Daffodils light up in the sun.

The curtain of cloud at the gateway
of the garden path begins to shift:
have pity for childhood,
the way of illusion.

Late at night,
the candle gutters.
In some distant desert,
a flower opens.

And somewhere else,
a cold aster
that never knew a cassava patch
or gardens of areca palms,
never knew the joy of life,
at that instant disappears-

man's eternal yearning."
Thich Nhat Hanh

"Drink your tea slowly and reverently,
as if it is the axis
on which the world earth revolves
- slowly, evenly, without
rushing toward the future;
Live the actual moment.
Only this moment is life."
Thich Nhat Hanh

"Be open, that is all."
Tao te Ching

"Walk and touch peace every moment.
Walk and touch happiness every moment.

Each step brings a fresh breeze.
Each step makes a flower bloom.

Kiss the Earth with your feet.
Bring the Earth your love and happiness.
The Earth will be safe
when we feel safe in ourselves."
Thich Nhat Hanh

"Like the empty sky it has no boundaries,
Yet it is right in this place,
ever profound and clear.

When you seek to know it, you cannot see it.
You cannot take hold of it,
But you cannot lose it.

In not being able to get it, you get it.
When you are silent, it speaks;
When you speak, it is silent."

Cheng-tao Ke

"When one comprehends nature
and understands the transformations,
one lifts the character to the level of the miraculous."

I Ching

When you observe nature's power
to transcend all obstacles,
you will discover
that this same power is inside of you.

Way of Tao

www.ingramcontent.com/pod-product-compliance
Lightning Source LLC
Chambersburg PA
CBHW032008040426
42448CB00006B/528